I0485257

MARKET YOUR MUSIC ONLINE

a workbook for musicians

by katherine forbes of designing the row

THIS WORKBOOK BELONGS TO

IF FOUND, PLEASE CONTACT

Market Your Music Online | 2nd Edition
Copyright © 2017 by Katherine Forbes of Designing the Row.
All rights reserved.

www.designingtherow.com
www.musicbizbesties.com

"People don't buy what you do,
they buy why you do it."

- simon sinek

INTRODUCTION

Welcome to the *Market Your Music Online* workbook! I am so excited that you are committing to making the most of your online communications starting today! The pages of this workbook are filled with words I hope will inspire you to authentically create and perpetually grow an online fan base you love interacting with!

If you take this workbook to heart, I know you will come away with marketing clarity, over one hundred social media ideas *(seriously, I counted!)*, and various materials for tracking your online growth and progress.

Before getting started, I need you to make me a few promises...

Promise to give the pages of this workbook your all.

Promise to fill in the blanks with truth and honesty.

Promise to be authentic while sharing the message of your music.

Promise to always continue creating your best work and never give up.

MEET KATHERINE

I love music... and I love helping others successfully share their music online.

katherine forbes
@designingtherow

This workbook is a collection of resources I have created throughout my time working in artist management, event planning, web design, and marketing in the Nashville music industry.

I constantly come across talented musicians but then come to find they have no online presence to back up their amazing music. So, I've written this workbook as a guide to benefit as many artists as possible!

Whether you're a new college grad or a Grammy Award winning band on a record label... let ***Market Your Music Online*** become your go-to online marketing planner and resource.

I can't wait to see what you make happen, in music and online!

HOW DO YOU STAND OUT?

It's simple.

All too easily we fall into the social media comparison trap *(yes, I'm guilty of this too)*. We stack up how many followers we have against others who are on a similar journey. *How many likes did their post get? How many shares did their music video get? How many comments did they get?*

Sound familiar? Do you want to know what the online marketing secret is? *(of course you do, that's why you bought this book!)*

People buy people, and they want to see the true you!

And **that** is how you stand out through online marketing... by being uniquely you. How cool is that?

So stop. Stop comparing your musical journey to someone else's social media feed. It's not helping you grow. Writing down dreams and goals on the other hand, **will** help inspire you to grow!

On the next two pages you have my permission to **dream big**! Once you put those big and scary goals of yours down on paper, you'll find them much less intimidating... I promise.

These next 2 pages set the tone for what you will accomplish with this workbook. If it makes you a little uncomfortable -- you're doing it right. Just remember to take your time and be true to yourself!

DEFINE YOUR GOALS

Let's dig in! Do you feel like you are on a never-ending journey to gain more followers, to make more money with your music, to book more shows? Use the space below to **define your top five goals**.

Make sure you are as specific as possible. You can't reach a goal if you do not clearly define it. *"Gain more followers"* does not count as a specific goal because it is open ended and too vague. *"Gain 600 followers on Facebook in the next 6 months"* is an attainable goal that you will be able to create actionable steps to reach.

1

2

3

4

5

Now that you have spent some time defining your specific goals, let's go even deeper.

Why do you want those followers, that money, or to play more shows? Gaining followers for the purpose of higher numbers will not help your music career until you can speak to the underlying **why**. *"Gaining followers so I can spread the message of my music to help heal those with broken hearts"* is what will make your music career stand out from the rest! For each goal you have on the previous page, I want you to now give it a **why**.

1

2

3

4

5

GO FOR IT

Of those five goals, which one is the biggest? **The one that you almost didn't write down because it scares you a little bit**... yeah, that one! Write it down again here.

dream big

[ ]

How would it make you feel to accomplish this goal?

[ ]

What can you do today to take a step towards achieving this goal?

[ ]

What can you do this month to get closer to this goal?

[ ]

How are you going to celebrate when you accomplish this big dream?

[ ]

MARKETING RULE #1

Before posting on social media,
always ask yourself "does this post
stay true to my goals and
why I make music?"

[**Hint:** If the answer is no,
reconsider sharing!]

WHO ARE YOU TALKING TO?

Do you ever have a hard time coming up with what to post on social media?

Do you ever run out of things to say to your best friend?

Well, have you ever thought of your followers as your best friends?

Your social media followers are your biggest fans.
They want to see you succeed.
They want to know what you're up to.
They want to feel like they know you on a personal level.
They are excited to be part of your journey!

So, next time you're writing a post or tweet and blank on what to say, just imagine how you might say it to your best friend!

And remember, social media is supposed to be **social**. Don't talk **at** your followers, talk **to** them and encourage them to respond!

This section will guide you through detailed questions so you can figure out exactly who your ideal fan is! If you spend some time with these questions and get to really know your target audience, your social media engagement will definitely benefit! Not only will you see more interaction, but it will become easier to attract and continue to build **your perfect audience**.

MARKETING RULE #2

When creating copy for social
media, your website, and emails
-- always write with your ideal fan
in mind!

[**Hint:** The more specific you can
be, the easier it will be to attract
the perfect audience!]

FIND YOUR AUDIENCE

Defining your goals is the first step towards finding your target audience. Now that you have clearly defined what you want to achieve -- let's talk about who you're marketing to!

Before we work on finding your target audience, we need to **define your current audience** so you can pin point any areas need that might need to grow and/or change. Use the space below to **describe your typical fan**.

Now, answer the following questions to **define your ideal fan**.

How old are they?

Mostly male or female? Single or married?

Where do they live?

What do they like to do in their free time?

Where do they shop?

What magazines and blogs do they read?

Where do they hang out online?

Do they work? Go to school?

What is their profession and income level?

More about your ideal fan!

Compare your typical fan to your ideal fan. How can you focus on growing your target audience?

WHY DO YOU HASHTAG?

I used to think people who used more than 2 or 3 hashtags on Instagram were just begging for likes. *And maybe that really is the case sometimes.* But, when I realized there was a hashtag world beyond #goals and #music, everything changed.

Hashtags are a way to connect with people who share similar ineterests!

Take a minute right now to write down the last 10-20 hashtags you used on socials.

Instagram (most important)

```

```

Twitter

```

```

Facebook

```

```

Looking at your list, do you think your ideal fan can you?? **#hashtagsarenotforrunonsentences**

SOCIAL MEDIA CHALLENGE #1

What Instagram hashtags does
your ideal fan use? Make a list
on the next page & start using the
hashtags in **your** captions!

RECOMMENDED HASHTAGS

I can't wait to meet you, and I hope you'll connect with me on social media! I'm **@designingtherow** on Instagram, Facebook, Twitter, and Pinterest!

Music Related Hashtags

#musicbizbesties
#girlswithguitars
#supportlivemusic
#musiccity
#musicrow
#instamusic
#musicgram
#indieartist
#acousticguitar
#writersround
#musicquotes
#supportlocalbands

#singersongwriter
#communityovercompetition
#newmusic
#nashvillemusic
#albumrelease
#recordingstudio
#womeninmusic
#womenincountry
#songwriter
#originalmusic
#tourlife
#musicscene

My Hashtags

MARKETING RULE #3

Keep all of your handles
the same so when you share
across platforms the links
will continue to work.

[It is also easier to remember
everything that way!]

HOW DO YOU KEEP TRACK?

There are a lot of online platforms and accounts to keep up with so use these next few pages to keep track of your logins and passwords!

Facebook

Twitter

Instagram

YouTube

Website

_____

Tip Paper clip this section so it is easy to find!
PS Use the blanks to add your airline accounts, merch store, & email logins.

TRACK YOUR PROGRESS

You can only see how far you've come if you keep track of where you started!

Use the next three pages as a social media count grid. Each week, mark the date and how many followers you have on each platform. If you did something notable (like a tv or radio appearance or a new album or music video release) make sure to keep track of those accomplishments as well.

I also recommend keeping track of these counts digitally as well. I use Google Sheets and have running tabs in the same sheet for each year!

So, while it may feel like your Facebook following is inching along, once you have several months of counts documented - I think you will be happily surprised by your progress!

The Social Media Counts spreadsheet will keep track of everything *you* want your fans to see, but do you actually know what someone sees when they Google you? The second spreadsheet will help you keep track of those results.

Google yourself today and write down the top 10 results. Maybe your old MySpace profile will come up, or an abandoned music profile from high school. Those results are **not** what you want your audience to see! Once you see your results, make some goals to be more active on the platforms that you'd like to rank higher in the search results! *(And maybe figure out how to delete that dang MySpace profile!)*

SOCIAL MEDIA COUNTS

Date

Facebook	Twitter	Instagram	YouTube	Spotify	Email List	Bandsintown		

Date

Facebook	Twitter	Instagram	YouTube	Spotify	Email List	Bandsintown		

Date

Facebook	Twitter	Instagram	YouTube	Spotify	Email List	Bandsintown		

Date

Facebook	Twitter	Instagram	YouTube	Spotify	Email List	Bandsintown		

Date

Facebook	Twitter	Instagram	YouTube	Spotify	Email List	Bandsintown		

Date

Facebook	Twitter	Instagram	YouTube	Spotify	Email List	Bandsintown		

Date

Facebook	Twitter	Instagram	YouTube	Spotify	Email List	Bandsintown		

Date

Facebook	Twitter	Instagram	YouTube	Spotify	Email List	Bandsintown		

Date

Facebook	Twitter	Instagram	YouTube	Spotify	Email List	Bandsintown		

Date

Facebook	Twitter	Instagram	YouTube	Spotify	Email List	Bandsintown		

Date

Facebook	Twitter	Instagram	YouTube	Spotify	Email List	Bandsintown		

Date

Facebook	Twitter	Instagram	YouTube	Spotify	Email List	Bandsintown		

Date

Facebook	Twitter	Instagram	YouTube	Spotify	Email List	Bandsintown		

Date

Facebook	Twitter	Instagram	YouTube	Spotify	Email List	Bandsintown		

Date

Facebook	Twitter	Instagram	YouTube	Spotify	Email List	Bandsintown		

Date

Facebook	Twitter	Instagram	YouTube	Spotify	Email List	Bandsintown		

Date

Facebook	Twitter	Instagram	YouTube	Spotify	Email List	Bandsintown		

Date

Facebook	Twitter	Instagram	YouTube	Spotify	Email List	Bandsintown		

GOOGLE SEARCH YOURSELF

Do you know what fans see when they Google you? Google yourself and write down the first 10 results below. If anything you see needs updating or editing, make notes and get to work! Make sure to check back in 6 months to see how the results change!

_____

TODAY'S DATE

1

2

3

4

5

6

7

8

9

10

6 Month Goals

```



```

6 MONTHS LATER

1

2

3

4

5

6

7

8

9

10

Before you fill out the next 4 pages, make a few copies so you can do digital reports on a monthly basis.

Website Analytics

If you don't already have a Google Analytics account or a way to track your website's analytics, you can create an account for free at analytics.google.com. Once you activate your account, make sure to analyze the **why** too - not just the numbers. When you write down the peak traffic date, make sure you also write down **why** it was a peak date. Did you send out an email that linked to your site that day? Or maybe you announced a tour? **These details are the most important part of analytics because you can't grow unless you know what works and what doesn't!**

Facebook Insights

Just like Google/Website Analytics, when you keep track of your Facebook Insights, always figure out the why! *Did you tour several cities during the past month and are they in your Popular Cities?*

Twitter Analytics

Twitter Analytics aren't as easy to find as Facebook's. Login to your account and go to analytics.twitter.com. There you will find several key metrics to help you improve on Twitter.

Instagram Insights

Connect your Instagram account to your Facebook Page and activate Instagram's Insights! Track your impressions, top posts, and see what time your followers are on Instagram!

WEBSITE ANALYTICS

Sessions & Users

Top Page Content

Peak Date(s)

Top Cities

Top Referral Sites

FACEBOOK

New & Total Likes

Largest Audience Demographic

Top Post: Description, Reach, Engagement, Reactions...

Popular Cities

Best days & times to post

TWITTER

New & Total Followers

Tweet Impressions

Top Tweet(s)

Top Mention

Top Media Tweet

INSTAGRAM

New & Total Followers

Impressions & Reach

Profile Views & Website Clicks

Top Posts

Best Times to Post

Top Cities

WHAT'S YOUR BRAND STYLE?

Visuals matter... a lot! When it comes to design, you need to be consistent and clear with your message. Think about Coca-Cola, Apple, or Gap... you know their logo and colors and can probably recognize their product without seeing a tag on it.

The same should apply to your music because you are a brand!

The next few pages will help you cover the basics, starting with hex codes!

Hex Codes

6 digit color codes. Visit color.adobe.com to upload an image and select your colors!

Fonts

Maybe this won't be something you will use, but you need to be able to communicate your style with future designers you hire. Think website, album artwork, posters, advertisements, t-shirts. You will want your font(s) to be consistent across all designs.

Style & Instagram Description Words

Do you like bold, feminine, dark, or monochromatic design? Words like these will help you communicate with designers and even keep you on track when picking an Instagram filter.

Mood Board

Keep clippings of pieces that reflect your style on the Mood Board page. Whenever you start to question your style, refer to this page!

DEFINE YOUR DESIGN RULES

Hex Color Codes

```
[                                        ]
[                                        ]
[                                        ]
[                                        ]
```

Fonts

```
[                                        ]
[                                        ]
[                                        ]
[                                        ]
```

Style Description Words

```
[                                        ]
[                                        ]
[                                        ]
[                                        ]
```

Instagram Mood Words

```
[                                        ]
[                                        ]
[                                        ]
[                                        ]
```

Mood Board (tape/glue color swatches, magazine cutouts, etc. here!)

WHAT AND WHEN SHOULD YOU POST?

I know you probably turned to this page for the magic answer... but there isn't one! *(Sorry!)* What and when to post depends on you and your audience!

Even though there is no magic time, I will tell you that you need to post the same content **multiple times**. In this section I give you 99 ideas for social media posts. Pick one topic you want to share (try a YouTube video or tour announcement) and **over the course of one day I want you to post:**

2x on Facebook
2x on Instagram
4x on Twitter (don't forget to RT others too)
1x in an email
1x as a news item on your website

Remember, be personal! Don't just blast your fans with a video, share a behind the scenes story or what the song means to you!

Topic to share

WHAT TO POST ON SOCIAL MEDIA

Most Importantly, Always...

1 Be yourself!!

2 Give credit when it's due (to photographers especially)

3 Have your ideal fan in mind, but...

4 Don't forget to communicate with the audience you have already worked so hard to grow!

Facebook

- [ ] **5** List your Music Page on your personal profile
- [ ] **6** Activate the Call-to-Action button
- [ ] **7** Post candid video content
- [ ] **8** Link to your website in your cover/profile photo descriptions
- [ ] **9** Change up your cover photo and profile picture
- [ ] **10** Double check the content in your "About" tab
- [ ] **11** Rearrange the navigation tabs to feature Tour Dates
- [ ] **12** Like and respond to fans' comments
- [ ] **13** Run a giveaway competition
- [ ] **14** Invite friends to like your Page
- [ ] **15** Use Facebook groups to connect with others
- [ ] **16** Target posts about shows to specific locations
- [ ] **17** Take advantage of Facebook ads
- [ ] **18** Analyze your insights to see what posts get the best response and create more similar content
- [ ] **19** Ask fans to add your Page to their favorites
- [ ] **20** Like & interact with Pages from your Page
- [ ] **21** Schedule posts in advance
- [ ] **22** Use the Bandsintown app for your tour dates

- [ ] **23** Use Facebook Live
- [ ] **24** Pin a post to the top of your Timeline (consider a video or post about your upcoming tour)
- [ ] **25** Post teaser content and link to your site for more
- [ ] **26** Share behind the scenes photos

Instagram

- [ ] **27** Link the profile URL to your subscribe / shop page
- [ ] **28** Create a consistent mood & color vibe
- [ ] **29** Start a hashtag for your band and encourage fans to use it at your live shows
- [ ] **30** Share a detailed story behind a photo
- [ ] **31** Ask questions to encourage comments
- [ ] **32** Share lyric graphics
- [ ] **33** Ask fans to tag their friends who live in cities where you're playing
- [ ] **34** Post pictures when you go to other artists' shows
- [ ] **35** Use the geotagging feature
- [ ] **36** Use the bio characters to explain the link you share
- [ ] **37** Grab viewers' attention in the first sentence of your caption so they'll click to read more
- [ ] **38** Hide hashtags in the 1st comment
- [ ] **39** Share others' photos and tag them in your post
- [ ] **40** Share videos using Instagram Stories
- [ ] **41** Go live and perform cover songs
- [ ] **42** Comment on posts of artists who have your ideal audience

YouTube

- [ ] **43** Activate your channel's homepage layout
- [ ] **44** Set up the "Featured Channels" sidebar
- [ ] **45** Add website and social media links in About tab
- [ ] **46** Create a new playlist and add it to your homepage
- [ ] **47** Add a channel trailer for unsubscribed visitors
- [ ] **48** Add videos from other channels to your playlists
- [ ] **49** Encourage subscribes, comments, and likes with video content, cards, or annotations
- [ ] **50** Link to other videos on your channel with Cards
- [ ] **51** Verify your website
- [ ] **52** Link to your website in video descriptions
- [ ] **53** Make sure your channel description is up to date
- [ ] **54** Create a YouTube ad
- [ ] **55** Do you have a separate VEVO channel? If so, create a VEVO playlist and add to your homepage
- [ ] **56** Update your Channel Art
- [ ] **57** Organize your homepage playlists and playlist video order in the order you want fans to watch
- [ ] **58** Post cover song videos
- [ ] **59** Perform on live stream
- [ ] **60** Collaborate with other artists to create videos

Twitter

- [ ] **61** Set your theme color to match your branding
- [ ] **62** Tweet to others and start a conversation!
- [ ] **63** Share lyrics and tag the artist and/or songwriter
- [ ] **64** Pin a tweet to the top of your profile

- [ ] **65** Post images directly to Twitter (instead of linking from Facebook or Instagram)
- [ ] **66** Use Canva to create the perfect size graphics
- [ ] **67** Participate in Twitter chats
- [ ] **68** Use hashtags
- [ ] **69** Search hashtags and reply to other users

Spotify

- [ ] **70** Embed your music on your website
- [ ] **71** Create playlists (not just of your songs)
- [ ] **72** Add the Spotify icon to your website
- [ ] **73** Check out your stats under the "About" tab
- [ ] **74** Follow other artists
- [ ] **75** Send tracks to friends (not just your music)
- [ ] **76** Share tracks to your other social media accounts

Email Marketing

- [ ] **77** Start a street team and send them special content
- [ ] **78** Send regular emails to your subscribers
- [ ] **79** Include social media icons and share buttons
- [ ] **80** Collect location information for email targeting
- [ ] **81** Take advantage of email analytics to see what works and what doesn't (hint: videos do really well)
- [ ] **82** Send free content to your subscribers
- [ ] **83** Offer limited time discounts to your online shop
- [ ] **84** Set up an automated email that sends to fans when they subscribe to your email list
- [ ] **85** Create consistency across all of your campaigns
- [ ] **86** Announce a tour exclusively to your email list

Website

- [ ] **87** Create a specific call-to-action on your homepage
- [ ] **88** Use the blog feature for recent news and press
- [ ] **89** Collect fan emails (refer to #80)
- [ ] **90** Link to all of your social media accounts
- [ ] **91** Make your most profitable content easily accessible on the homepage
- [ ] **92** Embed YouTube playlists on your media page
- [ ] **93** Embed Spotify albums & playlists
- [ ] **94** Add tour photos so site content is always fresh
- [ ] **95** Give people a reason to come back (new tour dates, news posts, special merch offers)
- [ ] **96** Add a favicon
- [ ] **97** Create moving content for visual interest
- [ ] **98** Share a preview of your email content and invite viewers to subscribe for more content
- [ ] **99** Host a pre-sale for an upcoming album or tour exclusively on your site

Notes & Ideas

"I got 99 problems, but social media ain't one!"

SOCIAL MEDIA CHALLENGE #2

Step out of the "me me me" mindset and share a friend's YouTube music video. Maybe they will even do the same for you in return! What a concept... I know!

#communityovercompetition

MARKETING RULE #4

Run Facebook ads and
sponsored posts only for content
that will bring in money.
No need to pay just for likes!

WHEN TO POST ON SOCIAL MEDIA

There is no "magic" time to post... because everyone's audience is different. But, thanks to social media analytic tools we can get a good idea as to when our followers are active!

Google Analytics

Facebook Insights

Instagram Insights

The more active you are, the more all the social media algorithms will favor your content!

If you want to take it to the next level, check out **Buffer.com**. Not only can you **schedule posts for all socials in one place**, but it also has a tool that let's you analyze the reach and impressions of each post.

IS YOUR YOUTUBE CHANNEL GOOD ENOUGH?

YouTube is the #2 search engine... while you can't practically post a new video as often as you post on other social platforms, make sure that your images, description, and links are all up to date!

Current # of subscribers & goals to grow

Collaboration ideas (songs and artists)

Cover song video ideas

Most popular video currently & ideas to create more like it

YouTube Search yourself... what are the top results?

15 STEPS TO A BETTER YOUTUBE CHANNEL

Channel Navigation

1 Hover under the right corner of your channel art

2 Click on the edit pencil icon

3 Click Edit Channel Navigation

4 Enable to customize layout of your channel & save

5 Set a video for returning subscribers

6 Set a video trailer for new visitors

Create Playlists

7 Click playlists on your channel navigation

8 Create new playlists (Pro Tip: You can add videos to playlists even if you didn't upload them)

Channel Sections

9 Click the Add a section button

10 Content > Playlists > Single Playlist

11 Layout > Horizontal Row

12 Choose a playlist > Select a playlist you create in step 7 (sometimes it takes a little time for the new playlists to show up, so just enter the playlist URL). Click Done and repeat to add other playlists.

About

13 Click About in your channel navigation

14 Add or update your channel description

15 Add links to your website and social media accounts under Links

SOCIAL MEDIA CHALLENGE #3

Engage with your YouTube subscribers!

1 Reply to comments

2 Comment on and favorite other videos

3 Add relevant videos from other channels to your playlists

4 Include a YouTube video embed in your e-blast

5 Embed a YouTube playlist on your website's media page

MARKETING RULE #5

Never ask people to sign up for your "newsletter." Newsletters are lame; I think we can all agree on that. Make your sign-up copy irresistible!

[**Tip:** offer a free song download!]

WHAT'S YOUR EMAIL CONVERSION RATE?

It has been said over and over that you need to grow an email list because it is ultimately the only thing you have complete control over.

It is also a big deal when someone allows you space in their inbox, so take advantage of that!

The people who sign up for your email list are your biggest supporters, so make sure to communicate with them and give them perks for signing up!

There are various ways to get your email sign up form in front of people... *hint: make it easy for them to find and subscribe!*

Ideas to grow your email list NOW

☐ **1** Activate your Facebook Call-to-Action for sign ups

☐ **2** Post your email sign up form and pin it to the top of your Facebook and Twitter profiles

☐ **3** Link to your sign up form in your website link on Facebook, Twitter, and Instagram

☐ **4** Include a link to your sign up form in your YouTube video descriptions

☐ **5** Add sign up to the header and/or footer of your site

☐ **6** Add a pop-up subscription box to a page on your site

☐ **7** Offer a free download in exchange for you fans' email addresses

☐ **8** Add a splash page to your website with only two options: "Subscribe" and "Enter Site"

COMMUNICATING VIA EMAIL

Every time you generate copy for an email, you need to have your ideal fan in mind. If you need a refresh, flip back to **Find Your Target Audience** (page 16).

Now ask yourself, do they read emails from their desktop or phone? Love free downloads? Shop online? What is their favorite social media platform? Do they watch a lot of YouTube videos?

Use this space to draft ideas for your next email series

MARKETING RULE #6

The more value you can add to your
email, the more likely people will
be to read and engage.

[**Tip:** Marketing content should
always be geared towards the
consumer.]

MARKETING RULE #7

Your email will get more opens if
you make the subject line
about the reader!

MARKETING RULES RECAP

Marketing Rule #1
Before posting on social media, always ask yourself "does this post stay true to my goals and why I make music?"

Marketing Rule #2
When creating copy for social media, your website, and emails, always have your ideal fan in mind and write to them!

Marketing Rule #3
Keep all of your handles the same so when you share across platforms the links will continue to work.

Marketing Rule #4
Run Facebook ads and sponsored posts only for content that will bring in money. No need to pay just for likes!

Marketing Rule #5
Never ask people to sign up for your "newsletter." Newsletters are lame; I think we can all agree on that. Make your sign-up copy irresistible!

Marketing Rule #6
The more value you can add to your email, the more likely people will be to read and engage.

Marketing Rule #7
Your email will get more opens if you make the subject about the reader!

SOCIAL MEDIA CHALLENGES RECAP

Social Media Challenge #1
What Instagram hashtags does your ideal fan use? Make a list to use in your posts!

Social Media Challenge #2
Step out of the "me me me" mindset and share a friend's YouTube music video. Maybe they will even do the same for you in return! What a concept... I know!
#communityovercompetition

Social Media Challenge #3
Engage with your YouTube subscribers! Reply to comments. Comment on and favorite other videos. Add relevant videos from other channels to your playlists. Include a YouTube video embed in your eblast. Embed a YouTube playlist on your website media page.

Key takeaways

MARKET YOUR MUSIC ONLINE
Copyright © 2017 by Katherine Forbes of Designing the Row
All rights reserved.

www.designingtherow.com
www.musicbizbesties.com

www.ingramcontent.com/pod-product-compliance
Lightning Source LLC
Chambersburg PA
CBHW021915170526
45157CB00005B/2078